# A Way of Life

Four Faith-Sharing
Sessions about
Sacrificial Giving, Stewardship,
and Grateful Caretaking

Joseph M. Champlin

**LITURGICAL PRESS**
Collegeville, Minnesota

www.litpress.org

Cover design by Monica Bokinskie. Photo by The Crosiers.

1     2     3     4     5     6     7     8

**Library of Congress Cataloging-in-Publication Data**

Champlin, Joseph M.
    A way of life : four faith-sharing sessions about sacrificial giving, stewardship, and grateful caretaking / Joseph M. Champlin.
       p. cm.
    Includes bibliographical references.
    ISBN 0-8146-3006-5 (pbk. : alk. paper)
    1. Catholic Church—Finance. 2. Christian giving—Catholic Church.
    3. Stewardship, Christian—Catholic Church. I. Title.

BX1950.C535 2004
248'.6—dc22

                                      2004002743

# Contents

# Acknowledgments

I wish to thank Peter Dwyer of Liturgical Press, my long time friends and colleagues, Francis (Dutch) and Barbara Schultz, as well as Lois Locey for their encouragement, guidance, and support of this project. All of them judged that a four-week small faith community sharing process on the topic of sacrificial giving, stewardship, and grateful caretaking was both needed and would be helpful.

We agree that following this Way of Life in any of these three forms requires an ongoing conversion or change of life. The booklet and process presented here have been designed to foster such a spiritual experience.

Parishes that have already implemented sacrificial giving, stewardship, or grateful caretaking should find that these four sessions will build on those foundations and strengthen or deepen them. Parishes now contemplating the introduction of any of the three approaches may also consider *A Way of Life* as a useful beginning step.

The statistics in Session 4 on the level of giving among American Catholics were taken from the *U.S. News and World Report* (December 4, 1995, "Who Gives What," 87) and the *National Catholic Reporter* (April 23, 1999, "Giving as a Percentage of Income," 8).

Leaders of Renew International—Msgr. Thomas Kleissler, Michael Brough, and Mary C. McGuiness, O.P.—originally proposed the possibility of such a small faith community sharing process on stewardship. They also encouraged a first draft of materials and offered invaluable suggestions on those developed. The present work represents an abbreviated, edited, and refocused version of that original product. I am deeply grateful to them for the energy they expended on this concept. Mr. Tom Green from the Basilica of Saint Mary in Minneapolis and Ms. Lois Locey of St. Michael's Parish in Olympia, Washington, were most gracious in sharing their impressive materials for fostering time and talent.

Friends as well as colleagues in the stewardship and sacrificial giving movement reviewed this manuscript and provided many useful insights. It is a better publication because of their comments and I am most grateful to them.

Finally, my appreciation to Mrs. Ann Tyndall who patiently and expertly transcribed my often illegible handwritten pages to the word processor and produced a readable text.

May the Lord touch the hearts of all those who move through these four sessions, deepening their faith, gratitude, and openness of heart, a deepening which will lead them to greater sharing of their time, talent, and treasure with and for others — thus making this a better world and building up the Church.

# Introduction

Faithful followers or disciples of Christ seek to observe a triple approach in their daily lives: they *believe* that everything comes from God; they express in their hearts and with words their *gratitude* for these gifts; they, with an openness of spirit, *share* a portion of these blessings with others to make this a better world and to build up the Church.

We generally categorize these gifts or blessings to be shared under the following headings:

**Time.** For many, at least in our western world today, time is often the most precious commodity we possess.

**Talent.** Our own unique and individual talents come ultimately from God and God's providence, but mediated through birth and nurturing, education and training, work activities and personal experiences.

**Treasures.** These financial resources available for sharing accrue from a variety of sources—children's allowances, part-time jobs, weekly paychecks, annual salaries, dividends, inheritance, social security benefits, winning a World Series pool. In a word, treasure is any income we receive.

That approach of faith, gratitude, and an openness of heart willing to share a portion of our time, talent, and treasure for others has been termed, among other titles, sacrificial giving, stewardship, or grateful caretaking. Followed faithfully, as one can see, it is indeed a way of life, not merely a needed program or even a once only process.

This booklet contains four small group faith community sessions designed to help participants understand better this particular way of life and apply it very personally to themselves. Each 60–90 minute gathering of 5–15 people includes: biblical passages and reflective prayer, brief instructions and fundamental concepts, and extended sharing and group discussions. We hope that during the days after each session participants will ponder the experience and change their lives accordingly. As a way of life, sacrificial giving, stewardship, or grateful caretaking does demand a frequent and ongoing conversion of the heart.

Session 1. "A Theology of Grateful Giving" develops the concepts outlined at the beginning of this Introduction. Three subsequent meetings cover: 2."Discerning My Gifts"; 3. "Sharing My Time and Talent"; 4."Taking a Step Toward Tithing My Treasures."

An Appendix contains Guidelines for These Sessions, the Plan for Each Session, Available Resource Materials, Sample Time and Talent Forms, and Four Hymns.

The Introduction to our American Bishops' pastoral letter *Stewardship: A Disciple's Response* clearly and succinctly summarizes that triple approach to daily life we have described:

> Disciples who practice stewardship recognize God as the origin of life, the giver of freedom, the source of all they have and are and will be. . . . They know themselves to be recipients and caretakers of God's many gifts. They are grateful for what they have and received and eager to cultivate their gifts out of love for God and one another.

# A Theology of Grateful Giving

**Gathering** (10).

[**Singing** (5). We stand and pray twice by singing three verses of "Where Charity and Love Prevail."]

**Reflecting** (10). We take our places, then prayerfully listen to and ponder these biblical passages:

Our dominion over creation (Genesis 1:26-28)
Caretakers of this world (Genesis 2:8–9:15)
On being grateful (Luke 17:11-19)
Faith and works (James 2:14-17)

**Learning #1** (5). We take turns reading this section:

---

In developing any theology we look to three sources for guidance and support: the Bible, the liturgy, and official church teaching. We follow that procedure at this section in our discussion of Grateful Giving.

**The Bible.** As we have just heard in the two creation accounts from the book of Genesis, God looks at the just-made, good, and wonderful world before our ancestors and charges them with the task of cultivating and caring for it. We are meant to be responsible caretakers of all God's creation.

**The Liturgy.** A revered Catholic truth states that the law of praying is the law of believing; the way the Church prays reflects what the Church believes. Our liturgy mirrors our creed; our worship expresses our faith. With that principle in mind we consider these phrases from prayers at Masses: "Almighty God, every good thing comes from you," and, "Source of life and goodness, you have created all things, to fill your creatures with every blessing." They also indicate that we are to "rule over all creatures." In summary, we are to view everything as a gift from God and use it well.

**Church Teaching.** At the Second Vatican Council in 1965, the bishops gathered in Rome declared: "It is for Christians a duty and an honor to give back to God a portion of the goods they have received from him." Three decades later, the *Catechism of the Catholic Church* states that the goods of creation are destined for the whole human race. It also cites St. John Chrysostom who said: "Not to enable the poor to share in our goods is to steal from them and deprive them of life. The goods we possess are not ours, but theirs."

Responsible caretaking means recognizing that all things are a gift from God and subsequently sharing a portion of these gifts with others, especially with those in need.

---

**Sharing #1** (15). We reflect upon the biblical readings and learning presentation in response to this question:

"What thoughts or feelings did the biblical readings and learning presentation trigger within you?" After a moment to reflect, we share our thoughts and feelings with a neighbor; later with all members of the group.

**Learning #2** (10). After an optional 60-second stand and stretch break, we once again resume our places and take turns reading this section:

---

Good stewards or responsible caretakers must possess in abundance three spiritual virtues or inner qualities: faith, gratitude, and openness of heart.

**Faith.** Faith, an inner quality and gift from God, is an attitude that, in the words of one bishop, "enables us to look beyond and see something more." We recognize the divine presence through many situations that, in turn, underscores our belief that everything is from above. Thus we discover God in:

*Beauty.* A contemporary writer remarks that beauty arrests us, stops us in our tracks, takes us out of our ordinary routine and leads us to transcendence, to God. In geographical areas with a pronounced change in seasons, the multi-colored fall foliage is a perfect example.

*Burdens.* A loving God brings good out of bad. During and after the darkness of 9/11, Americans discovered or rediscovered the critical importance and value of their close relationships.

*Coincidences.* Those many positive coincidences in our lives can be dismissed as purely accidental or signs of divine providence. Most engaged couples would attribute their initial encounter and the love which grew from it to the latter.

*Blessings.* When prayers are answered with a disease healed, problem solved, or dreams fulfilled, believers see the hand of God in that experience.

*Rainbows.* Many consider rainbows a sign of God's heavenly presence beside us on our earthly journey. They would look to the story of Noah, the ark and the covenant, with God's remark about a bow appearing in the clouds, as confirmation of this experience (Gen 9:14-17).

*Worship.* A Catholic theologian cites number 7 of the Constitution on the Sacred Liturgy from Vatican II as the doctrinal basis for the many worship changes we have experienced over the past three decades. The bishops assembled at Rome declared in this paragraph that to bring about the desired spiritual renewal of Christians and to carry out the lofty mission of the Church, "Christ is always present in his Church, especially in her liturgical celebrations."

Then in staccato fashion this paragraph lists the presences of Jesus in those sacramental actions. Christ is present in the

Eucharist, sacrifice, sacrament, and reserved in the tabernacle. He is present in the sacraments "so that when anybody baptizes it is really Christ himself who baptizes. He is present . . . when the holy scriptures are read in church . . . He is present when the Church prays or sings for he has promised 'where two or three are gathered in my name, there I am in the midst of them'" (Matt 18:20). It takes faith, of course, to look beyond bread, water, wine, oil, hands, words, and people to discover that unique presence of God in sacramental actions.

Faith, then, looks beyond or within these natural and spiritual experiences to discover the presence of God and recognize, even more fundamentally, that God is the giver of every good gift.

**Gratitude.** If with faith we view everything as a gift from God, then a constant inner spirit of gratitude for such gifts is the natural consequence. Faith-based people logically will be grateful persons, carrying within their hearts an attitude of thankfulness and expressing that gratefulness publicly as well.

Moreover, a spirit of gratitude deepens our realization that everything comes from God; thus it strengthens our faith. It also helps curb our self-centeredness. In addition, it warms the hearts of both the human gift givers and the human recipients. Being grateful, therefore, draws us closer to God, to ourselves, and to others.

Gratitude is a key and essential note in our Catholic Christian biblical and liturgical tradition.

The root meaning of "Eucharist" is to give thanks and the four New Testament descriptions of the Last Supper all contain that notion.

At other moments in his public ministry, Jesus himself frequently gave thanks to God and spoke of the need for gratitude on the part of his followers. At every Mass the priest re-presents the Last Supper and recites those words of thanks. Furthermore, he also leads the community present during the preface into expressions of gratitude. "Let us give thanks to the Lord our God." We respond that "It is right to give thanks and praise."

The priest continues: "Father, it is our duty and our salvation always and everywhere to give you thanks through your beloved Son, Jesus Christ."

**Openness of Heart.** Gifts from God, received in faith and with gratitude, are not meant to be hoarded or kept for our own use exclusively. Instead, we need to share a portion of those blessings from above to others, especially to persons in need. In that way we make this a better world and build up the Church. We could categorize those blessings or gifts under the title of time, talent, and treasure.

*Time.* In our high pressured, time conscious society, this may be the most challenging gift to share. That sharing can take, of course, an unlimited number of forms, from volunteer service at school or church to staffing a downtown soup kitchen or hospital gift shop.

*Talent.* This sharing likewise will occur in a countless variety of ways, from mentoring at-risk students in a center city school to serving on a financial committee for a non-profit organization, from using musical talents at church worship to staffing for several weeks a medical clinic in some Central American country.

*Treasure.* A portion of one's financial resources, ideally at least 10 percent or a tithe, goes to church and charity, building up the parish and making this a better world. The latter includes one's personal charities such as caring for an ailing relative, donations to the United Way, or support of missionaries.

In all these sharings, Blessed Mother Teresa of Calcutta, with her service for the poorest of the poor, gives us both a model and words of advice: "It is not what we do that is important, but the amount of love we put into the doing."

When we receive God's gifts and are willing to share a portion of them with others, we seem to flourish and to be full of life. When, on the other hand, we cling and do not share, we often appear to stagnate and become lifeless.

13

**Sharing #2** (20). We reflect and share our responses to these inquiries:

"Recall an instance in which you experienced the presence of God through beauty, a burden, coincidence, blessing, rainbow, or worship event." "Do you think we have lost the habit of gratitude in our lives?" "Cite an example in which you recently have shared your time, talent or treasure."

**Reading** (5). For our homework, we look up the designated biblical excerpts, reading the entire chapter with any footnotes from which they were taken. In addition, we continue to reflect on how the teaching about faith, gratitude, and openness of heart impacts our personal lives.

**Reviewing** (5).

**Praying** (5).

# Discerning My Gifts

**Gathering** (10).

[**Singing** (5). We stand and pray twice by singing four verses of "Lord, Whose Love in Humble Service."]

**Reflecting** (10). We take our places, then prayerfully listen to and ponder these biblical passages:

Called by name and precious in God's sight (Isaiah 4-3; 1-2; 4-5)
Important to God (Matthew 6:25-34)
One Body, many functions (1 Corinthians 12:24-31)
The ten talents (Matthew 25:14-30)

**Learning #1** (5). We read this section about discerning our gifts:

———

The biblical readings for this session teach us that we have been made by God, that each one of us is beloved, unique, and endowed with distinctive, important gifts or talents.

But what are these gifts or talents? More specifically, how do I determine what are my own distinctive gifts or talents, important for making this a better world and building up the Church?

Here are some methods which can help identify your gifts or talents:

1. Recall some activity, project or event at which you were very successful. What gifts or talents enabled you to succeed in this venture?
2. Reflect upon what you like to do and are good at doing.
3. Remember past positive comments of others who recognized some of your gifts or talents and praised you for them.

With these three steps of recalling, reflecting, and remembering in mind, spend a period of time in prayer, asking God the giver of every gift from above to help you discern what real and valuable gifts or talents you possess.

---

**Sharing #1** (15). We reflect upon the biblical readings and learning presentation in response to those three questions from the learning presentation and share them with another first and then with the group:

1. Recall in your life a successful activity, project or event.
2. Reflect upon what you like to do and are good at doing.
3. Remember how others have recognized a gift or talent you have.

We begin with number 1, "Recall," and, as time permits, then continue on with number 2, "Reflect," and number 3, "Remember." However, if sharing on "Recall" consumes all the time allotted, set aside some moments at home during the week ahead following through with "Reflect" and "Remember."

**Learning #2** (10). After taking an optional 60-second stand and stretch break, we once again resume our places and read this further presentation on discerning our gifts in relation to the need which the world and Church has for them:

---

Once we have identified some of our own gifts through personal reflection and group discussion, we then seek to match them with the needs of our Church and of the world around us. This matching fulfills two functions: it actually reinforces the identification of our talents and opens up possibilities for us to share those gifts for building up the Church and making this a better world.

We could place these possibilities for service or ministry into four categories:

1. **Within the parish.** This process of sharing naturally includes the parish to which we belong.

    Probably most parishes in the United States today feature annually some type of Volunteer, Time and Talent, Stewardship, or Ministry Weekend. During the course of those days, through pastoral reflections and personal testimonies at homily time together with printed materials and perhaps a Ministry Fair, parish leaders describe possibilities of service within the church community.

    Two parishes in this country have developed impressive materials for the recruitment of volunteers willing to share their unique gifts: St. Michael's Catholic Church in Olympia, Washington, and The Basilica of Saint Mary in Minneapolis.

    We have reprinted samples of their creative and thorough processes and materials in the Appendix.

2. **Outside the parish.** There are truly unlimited ways in which people use their talents in service of others outside the parish, either as paid employees or volunteer workers: men and women wait on tables in restaurants and distribute food at soup kitchens, help in hospitals and clerk at supermarkets, pilot airplanes and build Habitat for Humanity houses, counsel people in need and serve on Hospice teams, teach in schools and are active in politics, fund-raise for a symphony and fight fires for the city.

    They often may fail to recognize that their daily employment or volunteer efforts are actually ministries of service.

3. **In the workplace.** This somewhat indirect sharing of time and talent means using what we do or how we do it to transform by our Gospel values the atmosphere which

surrounds us. That may entail a warm smile or thoughtful deed, a positive conversation or serious intervention, a conscientious work ethic or creative project suggestion.

4. **Around the home.** We are called to care for and cultivate the creation God has given us. Within our households is the best place to begin becoming more conscious of the environment. Adults can teach young people by word and example not to waste, but to conserve and recycle, not to consume selfishly or carelessly, but to protect and preserve natural resources, not to litter, but to pick up. In summary, we are to be co-creators with God in making this a better, brighter, and more beautiful world.

---

**Sharing #2** (20). We reflect and share our responses to these questions:

   a. Identify one or a few ways in which you have shared your time and talent within or outside the parish. What has that experience or experiences meant to you?
   b. Reflect upon one way in which you have used your time and talent to make this a better and more beautiful world either in the workplace or around the home.

**Reading** (5). Once again, we read the entire chapter from which each biblical excerpt has been taken. Also, prayerfully discern your gifts and recommit to some current ministry in which you are already engaged or commit to a new sharing of your gifts.

**Reviewing** (5).

**Praying** (5).

# SESSION 3

# Sharing My Time and Talent

**Gathering** (10). We share our experience in response to these questions: "How did your homework go? Reading the entire chapters from which the four biblical excerpts were taken, further reflecting upon your gifts, and recommitting or committing to some ministry or service?"

[**Singing** (5). To prepare ourselves for the theme of sharing time and talent we stand and sing four verses of "Go Make of All Disciples."]

**Reflecting** (10). We take our places and prepare ourselves for prayerful reflection on these biblical passages about the nature of the Church.

As the Body of Christ (Acts 9:1-9)
As the Vine and the Branches (John 15:1-8)
As one but with many members possessing various gifts
(1 Corinthians 12:4-11)

**Learning #1** (5). We read this passage:

---

Three decades ago, a bishop spoke about the role of lay people in the Church today. He said to the assembled group: "We need you laymen and laywomen in a special way at this time in history. We need your gifts, your time and talent, your

19

active participation in the Church, because we have now and will have tomorrow fewer and fewer priests in the United States." His prediction has come true, of course, thirty years later. Over that period, sheer necessity alone impelled most pastors to hire staff or seek volunteers who could ease burdens caused by the rising number of parishioners and the declining number of priests available to serve them.

However, at the same time the bishop spoke about the necessity of lay involvement in Church activities, the Apostolic Delegate or Holy Father's representative in the United States, without denying the validity of the bishop's remarks, stated that even if there were an abundance of Catholic clergy, we should still be fostering the role of lay persons in our contemporary Church for spiritual reasons alone. As the saying goes, "We are the Church."

Here are a few of those spiritual reasons:

**The nature of the Church.** Whether viewing the Church as the Mystical Body of Christ or the Holy People of God, we believe that the Holy Spirit bestows unique gifts upon each member and by those graces empowers them to undertake various tasks and offices for making this a better world and building up of the Church.

**The Church's official teaching.** Three documents from the Second Vatican Council in the early 1960s provided explicit support for involvement of lay people in the activities of the Church: *The Constitution on the Church, The Church in the Modern World,* and *The Apostolate of Lay People.*

Recognizing the special gifts given by the Holy Spirit to lay people, the bishops then state that "there arises for each of the faithful the right and duty of exercising them in the Church and in the world for the good of (humankind) and the development of the Church."

The bishops become even more specific, mentioning such tasks as adopting abandoned children, assisting engaged couples in preparing for marriage, and sharing in catechetics or faith formation.

**The unique gift and call from birth and baptism.** Reflection on scriptural texts easily reveals just how unique and special each one of us actually is. From Isaiah 43, "I have called you by name: you are mine," to Matthew 6, "Look at the birds in the sky. . . . Are not you more important than they?" the same message emerges.

Human experience confirms this specialness. No one can duplicate another's fingerprints. There never has been, is not now, nor will ever be two persons exactly alike. Even twins differ. That means that through our birth we bring particularly unique and special gifts to our world and Church.

Through Christian Initiation by baptism, confirmation, and the Eucharist, God calls us to use these individual gifts for building up Christ's kingdom and enriching the Church. When we do so, the Church is more; when we fail to do so, the Church is less.

---

**Sharing #1** (15). Older members of the Church will recall when the clergy and religious performed most of the parish tasks. Today we see lay persons frequently fulfilling functions formerly cared for by the pastor or associate pastor. What are some of those previously clergy, now laity performed tasks? Identify particular gifts of time and talent needed to carry out effectively those responsibilities.

**Learning #2** (10). After taking an optional 60-second stand and stretch break, we once again resume our places and read this further presentation on time and talent.

---

**Time.** A recent survey revealed that the major challenges which married couples must work through during the first five years as husband and wife center around sex, money, and time.

One couple, he a lawyer and she a nurse, thought that after marriage there would be more time for each other. Instead, with their busy schedules, they struggle to find each day some quality "together time."

*Time* magazine published a cover story on, appropriately, the topic of "Time." It detailed the time pressures on Americans and the frantic search of many for free, leisure or relaxed moments. A suburban pastor finds it increasingly difficult to secure volunteers for needed tasks in his parish. With both parents often working, the children requiring transportation for a variety of activities, and school meetings or events demanding the parents' presence, time for them is a precious commodity, with little available for anything other than work and family.

As in the case with any limited resources, establishing clear priorities and making tough "no" decisions on certain time requiring activities not high on the priority list is critical for effective use of this limited resource and for the inner peace of any person.

There is, ordinarily, not enough time each day to do all the things we would like to do. There is, however, sufficient time to do daily what God wants us to do.

**Talent.** John Stopen is recognized as one of the most competent building engineers in the central New York area and across the state. Over the past eight years he has volunteered enormous amounts of energy as well as his expert talents on the repairs and restoration of our century-old cathedral complex that included dangling from a 100-foot device installing the support for a new ceiling-level sound system.

Helen Stier, in her late seventies or early eighties, served as the chief chef for a program which every Wednesday serves a hot breakfast to about one hundred homeless men. She would drive eight miles from her suburban home, arrive at the center around 4:30 A.M. and begin preparing the eggs, sausage, pancakes, or whatever was on the day's menu. She later would be joined by a corps of volunteer men and women who prepared toast, served the breakfast, washed dishes, distributed used clothing to the men, helped them obtain ID cards necessary for public assistance, and cleaned the hall afterwards.

Gerry McNamara loves basketball and clearly possesses a talent for the game. As a freshman student at Syracuse University and a member of its nationally top-ranked basketball team, he established a Big East Conference record in accurate foul-shooting.

How did he develop such a skill? By practice, practice, practice. As a young boy, he remained in the gym after the usual team workout, spending two hours there alone with his father shooting foul shots.

As in the case of John, Helen and Gerry, the talents we can share for making this a better world and building up the Church combine gifts inherited at birth, nurtured by others, developed through our own efforts and further enhanced by education and lived experiences.

It remains an ongoing challenge for us to share both our time and talent with and for others.

---

**Sharing #2** (20). We reflect and share our response to these two questions.

   a) Is the lack of available time a concern for you? If so, how do you manage that challenge?

   b) Can you think of someone in your experience, like the engineer, those in the breakfast program, or the basketball star with his father, who has been given a talent, developed this gift and used it well for others?

**Reading** (5). For our homework we look up the biblical texts and read the entire chapter from which they were taken. In addition, to stimulate your thinking and expand your vision, study the material on volunteers from the churches in New York, Washington, and Minnesota reprinted in the Appendix of this booklet.

**Reviewing** (5).

**Praying** (5).

# Taking a Step Toward Tithing My Treasures

**Gathering** (10).

[**Singing** (5). We pray twice by singing all three verses of "For the Healing," based on a traditional eucharistic melody familiar to older people.]

**Reflecting** (10). We take our places, then prayerfully listen to and ponder these biblical passages on sharing our treasure.

Jewish practice of tithing (Deuteronomy 14:22-29)
Joyful and generous giving (Sirach 35:6-9)
Jesus' warning about greed (Luke 12:15)
The early Christians (Acts 2:42-47)
A cheerful giver (2 Corinthians 9:6-8)

**Learning #1** (5). We read this section:

God's greatest original gift to the Jewish people was their land. They were to divide this wonderful blessing into eleven portions for the tribes of Israel, with nothing set aside for the Levites who would be supported in another way.

As we read, they were to take a tithe or 10 percent of their labor and return this in gratitude to God. Part of that tithe was for the support of the Levite or priest and the other portion for a grateful, joy-filled worship celebration.

Every third year the tithe was allocated for those in need, those with no land—orphans, widows and strangers as well as the Levites.

The book of Deuteronomy highlights this notion of God's giving and of our giving in response. Some form of the verb to give occurs 167 times in Deuteronomy, with God the subject of the verb on 131 of those occasions.

The relationship between God and the chosen people ideally was to follow this pattern: God blesses them with gifts. They, to acknowledge their dependence and gratitude, respond by a willingness to relinquish a share of those blessings with others. When they do so, God blesses them again; they then respond once more.

Some argue that Christ ignored or cancelled this process of the tithe. That seems hardly the case. As a faithful Orthodox Jewish person, Jesus personally would have learned and practiced tithing. Moreover, in an incident recorded by Matthew, he castigates scribes and Pharisees for an exaggerated externalism and absence of mercy, but warns them not to neglect the tithe (23:28).

In addition, Christ cautioned his hearers about greed, told them to serve the poor with generosity, and promised that if they first sought God's kingdom, they would receive what is needed and even desired.

The Acts of the Apostles tells us how the early Christians lived out this teaching by sharing. In addition, Paul praised those first believers for sharing their treasure with the needy in Jerusalem and reminded his listeners that God loves a cheerful giver (Acts 2:42-47; 2 Corinthians 9:6-8).

———

**Sharing #1** (15). We reflect upon the biblical readings and learning presentation in response to these questions:

    a. Do Catholics in general take the first portion of any treasure they receive (e.g., paycheck, dividends) and consciously, gratefully set it aside for making this a better world and building up the Church?

b. Does your parish reflect the image of the early Christian community described in the Acts of the Apostles?

**Learning #2** (10). After taking the optional 60-second stand and stretch break, we resume our places and read this section:

---

We here summarize the overarching guidelines and fundamental principles of sacrificial giving, an approach to grateful caretaking. It is not the only method of introducing or implementing this concept on the parish level, but it does enjoy a proven track record.

There are four overarching guidelines to sacrificial giving:

• It is a process, not a product. Experienced pastoral leaders maintain that it requires ten years of consistent education and formation to transform a parish into a significantly grateful giving community.

• Sacrificial giving is based not upon the need of a parish to obtain money, but upon the need of people to give a share of their treasures for the poor and the Church.

• The process depends mainly upon the testimony of lay people to motivate parishioners.

• The sacrificial giving approach seeks to form consciences, to provide guidance for individuals, to help people decide in their hearts what portion of their treasure they will give back to the Lord in gratitude.

There are four fundamental principles of sacrificial giving:

*Principle 1:* Give back to God in a spirit of grateful dependence a portion of everything that our Maker has given us.

*Principle 2:* See that the gift is a sacrifice, an offering within the church service that makes holy all the efforts and earnings of the past week as well as a donation that seems almost more than affordable.

27

*Principle 3:* Use regularly a parish envelope for the sacrificial gift.

*Principle 4:* Look to the biblical concept of tithing as a barometer, guideline, norm, measuring rod, or estimating level for determining the amount of this sacrificial gift which is to be placed in the weekly envelope.

A tithe is 10 percent of one's gross income—ten cents of every dollar earned or received. That 10 percent is usually divided in this way: Half is placed in the parish's collection; the other half is set aside for the world's poor—a generic term that includes diocesan collections, the missions, local appeals for the needy and private charities. Some would also include Catholic school tuition in that second half of the tithe.

Few Americans and fewer Catholics practice the 10 percent or 5 percent figure of tithing, at least if we consider statistics over the past decade:

• Americans on an average contribute to church and charity, not church alone, from a low of 1.1 percent to a high of 3.2 percent. Interestingly, the persons with below poverty level incomes donate 2.7 percent.

• Among religion affiliated and non religion affiliated people, Catholics rank lowest in donations to charity and church ($508.00 annually), with people of no religion even higher ($848.00 per annum).

• Percentage wise among denominations, Latter Day Saints top the list at nearly 7 percent, Black Baptists in the middle at about 2.5 percent and Catholics at the bottom with approximately 1.2 percent.

Most of us, then, are not at the 5 percent parish level or 10 percent total plateau. The "Taking a Step" process, however, keeps the goal of tithing before us, yet makes it realistically possible to move toward that ideal. "Taking a Step" works this way:

• Identify your current income level on the chart on page 29.

• Move to the right on the same line to determine the amount you currently give weekly to the parish. Move directly

# TAKING A STEP TOWARD SACRIFICIAL GIVING

Challenge yourself to give an equal percentage to other charities. For example, if you're giving 5 percent to the parish, give an additional 5 percent to other charities for 10 percent total giving. Other charities might include homeless shelters, food banks, United Way, missions, schools, Catholic Charities, diocesan appeals, and your own personal support for an individual or several persons in need.

| Current Household Income | | | | Weekly Gift to the Parish (Rounded to the nearest $) | | | | | | | | |
| Hourly | Weekly | Monthly | Yearly | 1% | 1.5% | 2% | 2.5% | 3% | 3.5% | 4% | 4.5% | 5% |
|---|---|---|---|---|---|---|---|---|---|---|---|---|
| $4.80 | $190 | $835 | $10,000 | $2.00 | $3.00 | $4.00 | $5.00 | $6.00 | $7.00 | $8.00 | $9.00 | $10.00 |
| 7.20 | 290 | 1,250 | 15,000 | 3.00 | 4.00 | 6.00 | 7.00 | 9.00 | 10.00 | 12.00 | 13.00 | 14.00 |
| 9.60 | 385 | 1,665 | 20,000 | 4.00 | 6.00 | 8.00 | 10.00 | 12.00 | 13.00 | 15.00 | 17.00 | 19.00 |
| 12.00 | 480 | 2,085 | 25,000 | 5.00 | 7.00 | 10.00 | 12.00 | 14.00 | 17.00 | 19.00 | 22.00 | 24.00 |
| 14.50 | 575 | 2,500 | 30,000 | 6.00 | 9.00 | 12.00 | 14.00 | 17.00 | 20.00 | 23.00 | 26.00 | 29.00 |
| 16.75 | 675 | 2,915 | 35,000 | 7.00 | 10.00 | 13.00 | 17.00 | 20.00 | 24.00 | 27.00 | 30.00 | 34.00 |
| 19.25 | 770 | 3,335 | 40,000 | 8.00 | 12.00 | 15.00 | 19.00 | 23.00 | 27.00 | 31.00 | 35.00 | 38.00 |
| 24.00 | 960 | 4,165 | 50,000 | 10.00 | 14.00 | 19.00 | 24.00 | 29.00 | 34.00 | 38.00 | 43.00 | 48.00 |
| 29.00 | 1,155 | 5,000 | 60,000 | 12.00 | 17.00 | 23.00 | 29.00 | 35.00 | 40.00 | 46.00 | 52.00 | 58.00 |
| 33.50 | 1,345 | 5,835 | 70,000 | 13.00 | 20.00 | 27.00 | 34.00 | 40.00 | 47.00 | 54.00 | 61.00 | 67.00 |
| 38.50 | 1,540 | 6,665 | 80,000 | 15.00 | 23.00 | 31.00 | 38.00 | 46.00 | 54.00 | 62.00 | 69.00 | 77.00 |
| 43.20 | 1,730 | 7,500 | 90,000 | 17.00 | 26.00 | 35.00 | 43.00 | 52.00 | 61.00 | 69.00 | 78.00 | 87.00 |
| 48.00 | 1,925 | 8,335 | 100,000 | 19.00 | 29.00 | 38.00 | 48.00 | 58.00 | 67.00 | 77.00 | 87.00 | 96.00 |
| 57.70 | 2,308 | 10,000 | 120,000 | 23.00 | 35.00 | 46.00 | 58.00 | 69.00 | 81.00 | 92.00 | 104.00 | 115.00 |
| 72.10 | 2,885 | 12,500 | 150,000 | 29.00 | 43.00 | 58.00 | 72.00 | 87.00 | 101.00 | 115.00 | 130.00 | 144.00 |

up the chart to identify the percentage of income your current level of parish giving represents.

• Consider moving a column or two to the right as a step toward the tithing goal. For example, from 1 percent to 1.5 percent or 2 percent.

• Make a promise to yourself that you intend to maintain this new level of sacrificial giving during the next year.

---

**Sharing #2** (20). We reflect and share our responses to these questions:

Take a moment to identify your own personal or family percentage or level of giving to church and charity. Reflect upon what you have heard and experienced during these sessions. Consider raising your grateful gift of treasure 1/2 percent or 1 percent. (5)

As our four sessions come to a conclusion, take a moment to recall a point or two which struck you, moved you, perhaps impacted your thinking and even inspired a change in the way you hope to share your time, talent, and treasures with and for others.

Communicate your reflections to a person next to you.

If you care to do so, share those conclusions with the entire group. (15)

**Reading** (5). In addition to reading the entire chapters from which the biblical excerpts were taken, discuss with those in your household the practical sharing of time, talent, and treasure you hope to implement, especially as those steps may affect them.

**Reviewing** (5). As these sessions now conclude, each person should have an opportunity to respond to this question: What is your reaction to and how do you feel about these four sessions on Sacrificial Giving, Stewardship, or Grateful Giving as a way of life?

**Praying** (5).

# Appendix

## Guidelines for These Sessions

### Hospitality and Environment

Gathering as a small community to share life and faith is an important aspect of parish life. These will be sacred moments. When you come together, it is important that you take time to get to know one another. Therefore, in the first session particularly, begin with introductions. In subsequent weeks, if you have anyone new to the small community, again take the necessary time for introductions. It will also help you to get to know one another if you take about 10 minutes at the start of each session to talk a little about what has happened during the week.

Hospitality and environment are very important to the small community process. Each participant should possess a heart open to the others and to any newcomers. When possible, try to create a reflective environment with as few distractions as possible. You may even want to have a candle where you gather in order to create a prayerful atmosphere.

### Bible

While not essential, having the same Bible will nevertheless facilitate the process for reflecting at each session. Its presence and use week after week, at the sharing and in one's home, will be a sign of God's word in this process. We have provided details in the Resources section at the end of this booklet about the availability of a very suitable *New American Bible* paperback edition at a reasonable rate through quantity purchase.

Reading at home after each session the entire chapter from which the biblical excerpts have been taken, including any footnotes there, places the text in its proper context and gives it a wider as well as richer meaning.

### Length

The suggested time for each gathering is about 90 minutes. Session 1 may require an extra half hour to give time for introductions and reading of the introductory materials. It is important to have a balance of prayer, reflection, sharing, and talking about how we are living our faith. The numbers in parenthesis after the title for each segment gives an approximate amount of time to be allocated for every section. However, it is important to be flexible. Moreover, when necessary the sessions could be reduced to about an hour.

### Silence and Sharing

Silence is also an important part of the small community process. After the learning segments, take a moment before beginning sharing. Generally, the sharing time is about 40 minutes. This will give each person who wishes to share the opportunity to do so. It will be important for the community to recognize that each person needs the opportunity to share; therefore, no one person should dominate. Also, no one needs to share unless he or she wants to do so; there always must be a "free to pass option." It is important for the community as a whole as well as the leader to be aware of the balance in sharing.

### Living Out the Sharing

One of the key components of faith sharing is how we take what we hear and share, then live it out in our own lives. Therefore, each week offers an opportunity to make a commitment to live our faith and then to share how we did with that commitment the following week. We live in a hectic, busy world, so taking time for additional activities is not always easy. This may be a good time, however, to reassess our priorities and how we are living our faith in our activities. We may want to change some of those activities. In addition, we may need to look at how we are living our faith in the totality of our life: in our families, in our relationships, in our environment. We may not need to do more; we may need to do less. This is a time to look at how we are living the values of Jesus and perhaps to identify new behaviors and attitudes.

### Socialization

A wise pastoral leader, fond of brief and direct words of wisdom, once suggested: "When you meet, eat." Some simple refreshments after the formal session could be helpful in building a close bond among participants.

### Leader

The leader of a Small Faith Community Sharing Session is not a theologian with answers, or a counselor who seeks to solve problems, or a teacher with expertise on the topics of sacrificial giving, stewardship, or grateful caretaking. Rather, the leaders are facilitators who warmly welcome individuals, help build a community through gracious hospitality, and guide participants through the process detailed in this booklet.

## The Plan for Each Session

**Gathering** (10). For the first session (and perhaps the second) name tags would be helpful and, of course, introductions with a little background of each participant. A little time might also be spent in response to the following question: "What led you to join this faith-sharing process and what do you hope to gain from it?" During sessions, the Gathering segment will be directed to another inquiry: "How did the last session impact your thoughts, feelings, and actions during the days afterwards?"

[**Singing** (5). This is an optional part of each session. Still, according to an ancient saying: when we sing, we pray twice. Moreover, singing helps to create a closer bond among people. At the back of the booklet we have provided a song or hymn which connects with the theme of each session. The music or melody will be familiar; the words may seem unfamiliar. We also usually sing better when standing.]

**Reflecting** (10). With a copy of the Bible on their laps and feet on the floor, participants sit erect and close their eyes. They take two deep breaths, become conscious of their thoughts and feelings, then reflect on Jesus' words: "Where two or three are gathered in my name, there am I in their midst," and, "If you believe in me, the Father and I will come and make our dwelling place within you." Each one silently asks for God's blessing on the small community and the session. Another deep breath and then all gently reopen their eyes and prepare to hear God's word.

All locate the passages and follow along as different persons read aloud the designated sections.

The leader invites them to reflect silently on the biblical passages for a minute or two. Then all recite together the Lord's Prayer.

**Learning #1** (5). Participants take turns reading portions of the first learning segment.

**Sharing #1** (15). After a brief period of silent reflection, the leader invites personal sharing about the biblical readings and learning presentation. Each person shares with a neighbor; after a sufficient period of time, individuals share their thoughts and feelings with the group. The leader may facilitate the process with these or similar words: "What thoughts or feelings did the biblical readings and learning presentation trigger within you? After a moment to reflect, would you share your thoughts and feelings with a neighbor?" The leader gives them about one minute for silent reflection, then encourages them to share. After several minutes, the leader invites them to share with the whole group.

**Learning #2** (10). (The group may wish to stand and stretch for sixty seconds at the conclusion of the first sharing session, then resume their places.) Participants take turns reading the second learning segment.

**Sharing #2** (20). The leader invites the group to share spontaneously in response to the questions provided. All read the questions, even taking time to read them aloud. The leader guides them through sharing on the questions one at a time. Flexibility is the key here. Sharing is the goal, not necessarily covering all the questions. For example, the first question may prompt a swift sharing and consume all the allotted time. Participants in that case can then reflect upon the other questions at a later occasion. It will be for the leader to make ongoing judgments about the process as the sharing unfolds.

**Reading** (5). The leader encourages participants as their "living out the sharing assignment" to read from the Bible the entire chapter from which the excerpts in the Reflecting segment have been taken. The leader also reminds them of the appropriate action decided upon.

**Reviewing** (5). The leader conducts a brief review or evaluation of this session. "What are your thoughts or feelings about this first session?" "How could we do things better at the next session?"

**Praying** (5). Conclude by invoking Mary, the Queen of Peace, and seeking her help through recitation of the Hail Mary. We ask that our hearts may be open to people throughout the world, especially those in need, and that the hearts of terrorists may change.

Simple refreshments may follow the session.

### Resource Materials

*Bibles*

A St. Joseph's paperback version of the *New American Bible* (Book number 609/04), from Catholic Book Publishing Corp. (77 West End Road, Totowa, NJ 07512; Telephone: 973/890-2400; Fax 973/890-2410) features an attractive cover, small, but adequate print, ample footnotes, significant commentaries and, in case lots of 20, a very reasonable price of about $5.00 per Bible plus freight.

*Bishops' Pastoral Letter*

*Stewardship: A Disciples Response,* "A Pastoral Letter on Stewardship," Tenth Anniversary Edition. United States Conference of Catholic Bishops. USCBB Publishing (3211 Fourth Street, N.E., Washington, DC 20017-1194. Phone: 800/235-8722. Fax: 202/722-8709).

*Sacrificial Giving or Grateful Caretaking Manual*

*Grateful Caretakers of God's Many Gifts: A Parish Manual to Foster the Sharing of Time, Talent, and Treasure* by Joseph M. Champlin. Liturgical Press (Collegeville, Minnesota 56321. Phone: 800/858-5450; Fax: 800/445-5899).

*Leaflets*

*Grateful Giving, Taking a Step,* and *El Dar Con Sacrificio* by Joseph M. Champlin. Available in packets of 100 from the Liturgical Press (see above).

## Time and Talent Sample Forms

The following samples of actual parish forms designed to enlist the time and talent of members for service in multiple ministries may help stimulate and widen the reflection of participants in the *A Way of Life* process.

1. *Cathedral Syracuse New York.* Sample can be found on page 37.

*Sample Volunteer Form*

## Volunteer Form

**Name** _____

**Mailing Address** _____

**Street Address** _____

**Envelope Number** (if applicable) _____

**Phone Number** (home) _____

**Phone Number** (work) _____

Mass usually attended (circle one):

Weekday 12:10 P.M.  Saturday 5:15 P.M.
Sunday 7:30 A.M.  9:30 A.M.  11:30 A.M.  5:10 P.M.

### Liturgy and Worship

____ Art and Environment
____ Young Altar Server (4th grade and up)
____ Adult Altar Server for funerals
____ Help with Friday Afternoon Novena to
Immaculate Conception 12:45 P.M.
    ____ Read prayers
    ____ Lead rosary
____ Friday Afternoon Adoration 1:00–2:00 P.M.
____ Usher
____ Greeter
____ Cantor
____ Choir 9:30 Sunday Mornings
____ Contemporary Music 11:30 Sunday Mornings
____ Instrumentalist

### Religious Education

____ Sunday Breakfast Program 10:30–11:30 A.M.
____ One to One Marriage Preparation
____ Wedding Rehearsal Coordinator
____ Rite of Christian Initiation of Adults
    ____ Host
    ____ Testimony
____ Door monitor Sunday 10:45–11:25 A.M.
____ Christmas Pageant
    ____ Costumes—Sewing
    ____ Help with children

### Young People

____ Youth Group Member
____ Adult Chaperone
____ Fri. morning after Thanksgiving sort and move
food to Downtown Service Center

### Pastoral Care

____ Special Minister of the Eucharist
(for the sick and homebound)
____ Nursing Home visitation
____ Help with semi-annual Anointing Service (Help
transport people or plan the liturgy)

### Service Programs

____ Brady Faith Center
____ Wednesday Morning Breakfast Program (Help
prepare and serve breakfast for men from a shelter)
____ Hungry and Homeless Dinners (Help prepare
and serve dinner on Sat. about 4–6 times a year)
____ Friendship club (Spend time with a group of
adults from the community with little or no social
or family support)
____ Jail Ministry Baked Good Sales (Sell these items
after Mass once a month—proceeds support Jail
Ministry)
____ Holiday Programs (Gift-wrapping, homebound
visitation, giving tree, addressing cards to shut-ins)
____ Downtown Emergency Assistance Program
(Occasional picking up of donations, but especially
needed at holiday time for preparing gift baskets)

### Cathedral School

____ Our school can use help in many ways. If you
are interested, contact Sr. Mary Jane (422-7217)
for ideas and to make arrangements.
____ Interested in Participating
____ Mentor

### Guardian Angel Society

____ Mailings
____ Phone Bank
____ Clerical Assistance (filing, computer entry)
____ Helping with Special Events

### Other

____ Cathedral Columns Newsletter (Bi-monthly)
____ Parish Life Committee
(Help plan and execute parish social activities)
____ Gift Shop Clerk (before/after weekend Masses
and Monday–Friday 11:15 A.M.–1:15 P.M.)
____ Baking Items for Youth Group Fall Bake Sale
(Proceeds fund youth activities)
____ Prayer Person for those in need
____ Administrative Help (mailings, clerical work, etc.)

### Ministries at Sunday, 5:10 P.M.

____ Lector
____ Eucharistic Minister
____ Server
____ Usher
____ Greeter

## 2. *Basilica of Saint Mary in Minneapolis*

The Basilica publishes creative and colorful materials describing many of its possibilities for sharing time, talent and treasure. One booklet "Whose Is It Anyway?" contains the Stewardship Report 2002, and lists alphabetically the names of 2,700 people who have served in one or several ministries during the past year.

A sturdy preliminary response card, ready for return mailing, indicates 45 possible "skills you would like to share" ranging from advertising and architecture through health care and housing assistance to videography and web page design.

A series of several glossy print, two-color texts describe in detail multiple opportunities for service under Administration, Basilica Development, Faith Formation Ministries, Pastoral Care, Social Ministry, Volunteer Ministry and finally, Worship and Sacred Arts.

## Time & Talent
# Response Card

There's more to stewardship than putting your envelope in the basket at Mass. Stewardship means giving of your time and talent as well as your treasure. If you have skills or interests that you feel may be of use to the Basilica, or if there are programs and ministries in which you'd like to be involved, please fill out this form and return by mail or drop it off at the Rectory or the Information Desk.

Place
Stamp
Here

BASILICA OF SAINT MARY
P.O. BOX 50010
MINNEAPOLIS, MN 55405-0010

## Sample Response Card

| Name |
|---|
| |

| Address |
|---|
| |

| City                          State                    ZIP |
|---|
| |

| Day Phone        Evening Phone |
|---|
| |

| E-mail |
|---|
| |

## Skills that you would like to share

___Advertising

___Architecture/Construction

___Art History

___Bible study facilitator

___Calligraphy

___Carpentry

___Childcare

___Clerical Skills

___Computer Skills

___Consultant

   (marketing/sales/financial)

___Cooking

___Copy writing

___Credit counseling

___Data entry

___Dentistry

___Electrical Skills

___Entertainer

___ESL tutor

___Fine arts

___Gardening

___Graphic design

___Health care

___Household assistance

___Language

   (proficiency/translating)

___Legal assistance

___Mailings

___Marketing

___Mentor

___Moving resources

   (help, vehicles, storage)

___Museology

___Music-voice/instruments

___Painting

___Phone work

___Photography

___Plumbing

___Proofreading

___Resume writing

___Retail sales

___Sewing

___Sign making

___Spiritual director

___Teaching/tutoring

___Trainer/facilitator

___Videography

___Web page design

## Ministries or programs of interest to you:

_____

_____

_____

_____

| OFFICE USE ONLY |
|---|
| Inquiry: |
| Data entry: |
| Letter: |

*The Basilica of Saint Mary thanks you for your commitment!*
*If you have questions, please call Sue Hayes: 123-456-7689.*

*Please fold and tape before mailing*

3. *St. Michael's Catholic Church in Olympia, Washington*
This parish has created its own Gift Inventory with permission of Augsburg Fortress for adaptation of material taken from *Created and Called: Discovered Our Gifts for Abundant Living* by Jean Morris Trombauer.

Their three-page form, "Discovering the Gifts Within You," features seven procedures to help individuals prayerfully discern their gifts, temperament, special passions, action styles, preferences, feelings about ministry, and availability or commitment.

## Sample Gift Inventory Form

**My gifts are . . .** Please place a ✓ check in the first column to indicate up to a dozen things that you do well. If there are other abilities that you would be interested in learning or having an opportunity to try out, place a check in the second column.

**First column:** I have developed a skill in...
▼ **Second column:** I have an interest in...
　▼

| | | |
|---|---|---|
| \_\_\_ | \_\_\_ | **Accounting/Finances** |
| \_\_\_ | \_\_\_ | Budgeting |
| \_\_\_ | \_\_\_ | Investing |
| \_\_\_ | \_\_\_ | **Archiving** |
| \_\_\_ | \_\_\_ | **Artistry** |
| \_\_\_ | \_\_\_ | Artwork |
| \_\_\_ | \_\_\_ | Calligraphy |
| \_\_\_ | \_\_\_ | Crafts |
| \_\_\_ | \_\_\_ | Decorating |
| \_\_\_ | \_\_\_ | Graphic Design |
| \_\_\_ | \_\_\_ | Interior Design |
| \_\_\_ | \_\_\_ | Painting |
| \_\_\_ | \_\_\_ | Photographing |
| \_\_\_ | \_\_\_ | **Athletics** |
| \_\_\_ | \_\_\_ | **Child Care** |
| \_\_\_ | \_\_\_ | **Clerical Work** |
| \_\_\_ | \_\_\_ | Mailing Preparation |
| \_\_\_ | \_\_\_ | **Communications** |
| \_\_\_ | \_\_\_ | Audio/Sound Systems |
| \_\_\_ | \_\_\_ | Recording |
| \_\_\_ | \_\_\_ | Telephoning |
| \_\_\_ | \_\_\_ | Video-Taping |
| \_\_\_ | \_\_\_ | Writing |
| \_\_\_ | \_\_\_ | **Computer Usage** |
| \_\_\_ | \_\_\_ | Data Entry |
| \_\_\_ | \_\_\_ | Database Applications |
| \_\_\_ | \_\_\_ | Desktop Publishing |
| \_\_\_ | \_\_\_ | Spreadsheet |
| \_\_\_ | \_\_\_ | Web Site Development |
| \_\_\_ | \_\_\_ | Word Processing |
| \_\_\_ | \_\_\_ | **Culinary Activities** |
| \_\_\_ | \_\_\_ | Baking |
| \_\_\_ | \_\_\_ | Cooking |
| \_\_\_ | \_\_\_ | Party Planning |
| \_\_\_ | \_\_\_ | Serving |
| \_\_\_ | \_\_\_ | **Driving** |
| \_\_\_ | \_\_\_ | **Facilities/Grounds** |
| \_\_\_ | \_\_\_ | Carpentry/Building/Construction |
| \_\_\_ | \_\_\_ | Gardening/Landscaping |
| \_\_\_ | \_\_\_ | Housekeeping/Cleaning |
| \_\_\_ | \_\_\_ | Maintaining Building/Grounds |
| \_\_\_ | \_\_\_ | Mechanical Work |
| \_\_\_ | \_\_\_ | Painting |
| \_\_\_ | \_\_\_ | Setting Up Rooms |
| \_\_\_ | \_\_\_ | **Faith/Spiritual** |
| \_\_\_ | \_\_\_ | Biblical Studies |
| \_\_\_ | \_\_\_ | Faith Sharing |
| \_\_\_ | \_\_\_ | Praying |
| \_\_\_ | \_\_\_ | Ritualizing |
| \_\_\_ | \_\_\_ | **Foreign Language—Specify:_____** |
| \_\_\_ | \_\_\_ | **Fund Raising** |
| \_\_\_ | \_\_\_ | **Helping** |
| \_\_\_ | \_\_\_ | **Hospitality** |
| \_\_\_ | \_\_\_ | Welcoming |
| \_\_\_ | \_\_\_ | **Group/Team Building** |
| \_\_\_ | \_\_\_ | Building Consensus |
| \_\_\_ | \_\_\_ | Coordinating |

**First column:** I have developed a skill in...
▼ **Second column:** I have an interest in...
　▼

| | | |
|---|---|---|
| \_\_\_ | \_\_\_ | Delegating (Letting Go) |
| \_\_\_ | \_\_\_ | Discussing |
| \_\_\_ | \_\_\_ | Facilitating |
| \_\_\_ | \_\_\_ | Leading |
| \_\_\_ | \_\_\_ | Negotiating |
| \_\_\_ | \_\_\_ | Organizing |
| \_\_\_ | \_\_\_ | Visioning |
| \_\_\_ | \_\_\_ | **Human Resource Management** |
| \_\_\_ | \_\_\_ | Recruiting Others |
| \_\_\_ | \_\_\_ | **Individual/Interpersonal Skills** |
| \_\_\_ | \_\_\_ | Interviewing |
| \_\_\_ | \_\_\_ | Listening |
| \_\_\_ | \_\_\_ | Mediating |
| \_\_\_ | \_\_\_ | Mentoring |
| \_\_\_ | \_\_\_ | Nurturing |
| \_\_\_ | \_\_\_ | Supporting (I'll Be There) |
| \_\_\_ | \_\_\_ | **Knowledgeable** |
| \_\_\_ | \_\_\_ | **Learning** |
| \_\_\_ | \_\_\_ | **Legal Services** |
| \_\_\_ | \_\_\_ | **Library Work** |
| \_\_\_ | \_\_\_ | **Management** |
| \_\_\_ | \_\_\_ | Analyzing |
| \_\_\_ | \_\_\_ | Problem-Solving |
| \_\_\_ | \_\_\_ | Researching |
| \_\_\_ | \_\_\_ | **Medical/Nursing Care** |
| \_\_\_ | \_\_\_ | **Music** |
| \_\_\_ | \_\_\_ | Music: Instrumental |
| \_\_\_ | \_\_\_ | Music: Vocal |
| \_\_\_ | \_\_\_ | **Pastoral Care** |
| \_\_\_ | \_\_\_ | Caring And Compassion |
| \_\_\_ | \_\_\_ | Visiting Others |
| \_\_\_ | \_\_\_ | **Performing** |
| \_\_\_ | \_\_\_ | Acting/Drama |
| \_\_\_ | \_\_\_ | Clowning |
| \_\_\_ | \_\_\_ | Dancing |
| \_\_\_ | \_\_\_ | **Program Development** |
| \_\_\_ | \_\_\_ | Discerning |
| \_\_\_ | \_\_\_ | Evaluating |
| \_\_\_ | \_\_\_ | Planning |
| \_\_\_ | \_\_\_ | Sharing Ideas/New Visions |
| \_\_\_ | \_\_\_ | Summarizing/Synthesizing |
| \_\_\_ | \_\_\_ | **Public Relations** |
| \_\_\_ | \_\_\_ | Marketing |
| \_\_\_ | \_\_\_ | Promoting Ideas/Ideas |
| \_\_\_ | \_\_\_ | **Sewing** |
| \_\_\_ | \_\_\_ | Mending |
| \_\_\_ | \_\_\_ | Quilting |
| \_\_\_ | \_\_\_ | **Social Justice Work** |
| \_\_\_ | \_\_\_ | **Speaking Publicly** |
| \_\_\_ | \_\_\_ | **Spiritual Vocation** |
| \_\_\_ | \_\_\_ | Priesthood |
| \_\_\_ | \_\_\_ | Religious Life (Sister or Brother) |
| \_\_\_ | \_\_\_ | Professional Lay Minister |
| \_\_\_ | \_\_\_ | **Teaching; Training** |
| \_\_\_ | \_\_\_ | **Working hard at what needs doing** |
| \_\_\_ | \_\_\_ | **Working With Children** |
| \_\_\_ | \_\_\_ | **Youth Ministry** |

## *Others would describe me as* . . . (✓Check up to five)

| | | |
|---|---|---|
| ___ authentic | ___ flexible | ___ patient |
| ___ compassionate | ___ friendly | ___ persistent |
| ___ cooperative | ___ happy | ___ reliable |
| ___ creative | ___ helpful | ___ resourceful |
| ___ diplomatic | ___ humorous | ___ team-player |
| ___ easy-going | ___ inclusive | ___ tolerant |
| ___ detailed-oriented | ___ industrious | ___ understanding |
| ___ efficient | ___ inquisitive | ___ wise |
| ___ energetic | ___ inspirational | ___ other:_____ |
| ___ enthusiastic | ___ open-minded | ___ other:_____ |
| ___ fair | ___ optimistic | ___ other:_____ |

The skills I would most like to develop further, the knowledge I would most like to gain, or the growth I would most like to experience by exploring my gifts include . . .

_____

_____

_____

## *My special passions at this time are* . . .

### Ministry areas within St. Michael Parish:

| | | |
|---|---|---|
| ___ aging | ___ finance | ___ stewardship: volunteerism |
| ___ arts | ___ grief ministry | ___ stewardship: sacrificial giving |
| ___ church at large | ___ missions | ___ singles ministry |
| ___ community outreach/service | ___ ministry in daily life | ___ small faith communities/groups |
| ___ ecumenism | ___ music | ___ spiritual growth & development |
| ___ education/formation: children | ___ new member welcoming/integration | ___ worship/liturgy |
| ___ education/formation: teens | ___ pastoral care | ___ young adult ministry |
| ___ education/formation: adults | ___ personnel/human resources | ___ other:_____ |
| ___ evangelization | ___ property management | ___ other:_____ |
| ___ family ministry | ___ sacramental preparation | ___ other:_____ |

### St. Michael ministries of outreach and other community ministries:

| | | |
|---|---|---|
| ___ abuse | ___ employment | ___ mental health |
| ___ addiction | ___ environment | ___ poverty and economic disparity |
| ___ the arts | ___ families & parenting | ___ prisons & rehabilitation |
| ___ care for and dignity of the elderly | ___ governmental & political reform | ___ public education |
| ___ child development | ___ grief & loss: life transitions | ___ refugees |
| ___ disabilities | ___ health care: illness | ___ self-esteem/actualization of |
| ___ discrimination (racial, gender, | ___ homelessness | children/adults |
| age, religious, etc.) | ___ human rights | ___ spiritual meaning |
| ___ economic & community | ___ hunger | ___ violence |
| development | ___ literacy | ___ other:_____ |

## The styles that best match my perception of myself include . . .

___ logical  
___ practical  
___ imaginative  
___ energetic doer  
___ makes decisions on facts  
___ makes decisions on hunches  

___ outgoing and gregarious  
___ reserved and reflective  
___ prefer open-ended flexibility  
___ prefer deadlines: specific tasks  
___ prefer harmonious environment  
___ prefer lively, open debate  

___ concerned with goals, outcomes  
___ concerned with relationships  
___ concerned with change  
___ enjoy starting things  
___ enjoy maintaining things  
___ enjoy finishing things  

## I prefer to minister in the following contexts . . .

___ with a large group  
___ with a small group  
___ with one or two others  
___ alone  
___ with ideas and data  
___ with things  
___ with people  
___ within our faith community  
___ within the larger church  
___ within the larger community  
___ in a mission setting in  
    another state or country  
___ other: _____  
___ other: _____  

___ with infants or toddlers  
___ with children  
___ with teens  
___ with young adults  
___ with adults  
___ with senior adults  
___ with singles  
___ with engaged couples  
___ with married couples  
___ with the divorced  
___ with the widowed  
___ with single parents  
___ with married parents  
___ other: _____  

___ with the ill  
___ with the dying  
___ with the grieving  
___ with the lonely  
___ with the poor  
___ with the hungry  
___ with the homeless  
___ with the unemployed  
___ with those in career transition  
___ with those in crisis  
___ with the addicted  
___ with the abused  
___ with the imprisoned  
___ other: _____  

## My feelings about being invited to minister at this time are . . .

___ anxious to learn and grow  
___ bored  
___ complimented; flattered  
___ curious  
___ eager and excited  
___ frustrated  
___ glad to use my gifts to serve  
___ never been asked  

___ reasonably comfortable  
___ reluctant  
___ tired and burned out  
___ uncertain and unsure of role  
___ unprepared  
___ worried or afraid  
___ other: _____  
___ other: _____  

## At this time, my preference is to participate in ministry opportunities that are . . .

___ a one-time commitment (1 hour to 1 day).  
___ a short-term commitment (up to 6 months).  
___ a specific, longer term of service (1, 2, 3 years, please specify: _____).  
___ I am able to commit: ___ hours per week ___ hours per month.  
___ I am available ___ Mondays ___ Tuesdays ___ Wednesdays ___ Thursdays ___ Fridays  
    ___ during the morning (9–12 noon) ___ during the afternoon (1–5 PM)  
    ___ early evenings (5–7 PM) ___ nights (7–9 PM).  
    ___ Winter ___ Spring ___ Summer ___ Fall.  
___ I prefer to serve ___ Downtown ___ Westside ___ Southside ___ No Preference.  
___ I am interested in becoming more involved. Notify me of opportunities that fit my gifts.  
___ I am interested in changing some of my current commitments.  
___ I am satisfied with my current involvements.  
___ I am unable to take on additional commitments at this time. Contact me _____ (when).  
___ I would like to talk with a member of the time & talent team about my gifts and calling.  

**St. Michael Catholic Church**  
**P.O. Box 766, Olympia, Washington 98507-0766**  
**Phone: (123) 345-6789 Fax: (123) 345-6789**  
**E-mail: Office@SaintMichaelParish.org**  
**www.SaintMichaelParish.org**

# Time & Talent
*Fostering Stewardship as a way of Life*

St. Michael's Gift Inventory was adapted for St. Michael Catholic Church, Olympia, Washington  
with permission of Augsburg Fortress from Created & Called: Discovering our Gifts for  
Abundant Living © 1998 Jean Morris Trumbauer (Draft 3/8/2000).

# Music

SESSION 1

## Where Charity and Love Prevail

1. Where char - i - ty and love pre - vail,
2. With grate - ful joy and ho - ly fear
3. For - give we now each o - ther's faults
4. Let strife a - mong us be un - known,
5. Let us re - call that in our midst
6. No race nor creed can love ex - clude,

1. There God is ev - er found; Brought here to - geth-
2. God's char - i - ty we learn; Let us with heart
3. As we our faults con - fess; And let us love
4. Let all con - ten - tion cease; Be God's the glo-
5. Dwells God's be - got - ten Son; As mem - bers of
6. If hon - ored be God's name; Our fam - i - ly

1. er by Christ's love By love are we thus bound.
2. and mind and soul Now love God in re - turn.
3. each oth - er well In Chris - tian ho - li - ness.
4. ry that we seek, Be ours God's ho - ly peace.
5. his bod - y joined We are in Christ made one.
6. em - bra - ces all Whose Fa - ther is the same.

Text: Based on *Ubi caritas*, 9th cent., tr. by Omer Westendorf, 1916–1997. Music: CHRISTIAN LOVE, CM, 86 86; Paul Benoit, 1893–1979. Text and music: © 1960, World Library Publications, 3825 N. Willow Rd., Schiller, Park, IL 60176. All rights reserved. Used with permission.

# Lord, Whose Love in Humble Service

1. Lord, whose love in hum-ble serv-ice Bore the
2. Still your chil-dren wan-der home-less; Still the
3. As we wor-ship, grant us vi-sion, Till your
4. Called from wor-ship in-to serv-ice, Forth in

1. weight of hu-man need, Who did on the
2. hun-gry cry for bread; Still the cap-tives
3. love's re-veal-ing light, In its height and
4. your great name we go, To the child, the

1. cross, for-sak-en, Show us mer-cy's per-fect
2. long for free-dom; Still in grief we mourn our
3. depth and great-ness Dawns up-on our hu-man
4. youth, the a-ged, Love in liv-ing deeds to

1. deed; We, your serv-ants, bring the wor-ship
2. dead. As, O Lord, your deep com-pas-sion
3. sight: Mak-ing known the needs and bur-dens
4. show; Hope and health, good-will and com-fort,

1. Not of voice a-lone, but heart: Con-se-crat-ing
2. Healed the sick and freed the soul, Use the love your
3. Your com-pas-sion bids us bear, Stir-ring us to
4. Coun-sel, aid, and peace we give, That your chil-dren,

1. to your pur-pose Ev-'ry gift which you im-part.
2. Spir-it kin-dles Still to save and make us whole.
3. faith-ful serv-ice, Your a-bun-dant life to share.
4. Lord, in free-dom, May your mer-cy know and live.

Text: Albert F. Bayly, 1901–1984, alt., © Oxford University Press. All rights reserved. Used with permission.
Music: IN BABILONE, 87 87 D, *Oude en Nieuwe Hollanske Boerenlities,* c. 1710.

## Go Make of All Disciples

1. "Go make of all dis - ci - ples": We hear the call,
2. "Go make of all dis - ci - ples": Bap - tiz - ing in
3. "Go make of all dis - ci - ples": We at your feet
4. "Go make of all dis - ci - ples": We wel - come your

1. O Lord, That comes from you, our Fa - ther, In
2. the name Of Fa - ther, Son, and Spir - it From
3. would stay Un - til each life's vo - ca - tion Ac -
4. com - mand; "Lo, I am with you al - ways": We

1. your e - ter - nal Word. In - spire our ways of learn -
2. age to age the same. We call each new dis - ci -
3. cents your ho - ly way. We cul - ti - vate the na -
4. take your guid - ing hand. The task looms large be - fore

1. ing Through ear - nest, fer - vent prayer, And let our
2. ple To fol - low you O Lord, Re - deem - ing
3. ture God plants in ev - 'ry heart, Re - veal - ing
4. us, We fol - low with - out fear. In heav'n and

1. dai - ly liv - ing Re - veal you ev - 'ry - where.
2. soul and bod - y By wa - ter and the Word.
3. in our wit - ness The Mas - ter Teach - er's art.
4. earth your pow - er Shall bring God's king - dom here.

Text: Leon M. Adkins, b. 1896–1986, alt., © 1964, Abingdon Press, admin. by The Copyright Company, Nashville, TN. All rights reserved. International copyright secured. Used by permission.
Music: ELLACOMBE, 76 76 D, *Gesangbuch de Herzogl*, Wirtemberg, 1784.

## For the Healing

1. For   the heal-ing   of   the   na-tions, Lord, we   pray with
2. Lead your peo-ple   in - to   free-dom, From de - spair your
3. You,   cre - a - tor God, have writ - ten   your great name on

1. one   acc - ord;   For   a   just   and   e - qual shar - ing
2. world re - lease; That   re - deemed from war   and   ha - tred,
3. hu - man-kind; For   our   grow - ing   in   your like - ness

1. Of   the things that   earth af - fords.   To   a   life   of
2. All   may come and   go   in peace. Show us   how through
3. Bring the   life   of   Christ to mind: That by our   re -

1. love   and ac - tion Help us   rise and pledge our   word.
2. care   and good - ness Fear will die   and   hope   in - crease.
3. sponse and ser - vice Earth its   des - ti - ny   may find.